THE GREAT SEA ISLANDS HURRICANE & TIDAL WAVE

A STORM OF POLITICS & CHARITY DURING THE JIM CROW ERA

By Craig G. Metts

Includes an Interview and Historical Perspective by
Noted USC Professor and Historian Dr. Walter Edgar

Published by Catmoon Media
Columbia, South Carolina

For Colleen, Dashiell and Desmond

CONTENTS:

FOREWORD...6

INTRODUCTION...10

THE STORM..16

THE AFTERMATH..24

THE RELIEF EFFORT...36

THE RED CROSS..44

POLITICS AND PUBLIC OPINION.......................56

ECONOMY..70

CONCLUSION..78

APPENDIX...82

BIBLIOGRAPHY..90

NOTES...96

FOREWORD:

Years ago, while searching topics for a college history paper, I came upon this small but very curious entry in The New York Public Library Book of Chronologies:

1893 - Tidal wave generated by hurricane hits U.S. southeastern coast, submerging islands between Charleston, South Carolina and Savannah, Georgia (August 27); 1,000 die.[1]

Being a native, with an intense interest in South Carolina and United States History from the Civil War to the Great Depression, I was dumbstruck. My curiosity was aroused because I thought I knew enough to know that could be no Tidal Waves along the South Carolina Sea Coast. At first I thought this entry was an error, or an inside joke. This belief was supported because of the simple reason that I could not find any other mention of a tidal wave hitting the seacoast in the current histories of South Carolina. I found small references and footnotes about a hurricane that struck the South Carolina Sea Coast in August of 1893, but no

---

[1] Wetterau, Bruce, ed., *The New York Public Library Book of Chronologies.* (New York: Simon & Schuster, Inc., 1990.) p. 519.

detailed accounts. Always ready for a good challenge, I took up the topic for my research paper. Eventually, I learned that the storm phenomenon was perceived as a tidal wave, because of the extreme storm surge, already on top of record high tides, so great that it completely submerged and demolished the South Carolina Sea Islands on the night of the 27th, August 1893.

The vast majority of the victims were Black Sea Islanders. Newly emancipated slaves and their descendents during a time of the "Jim Crow" and post-reconstruction era. One can only imagine the monstrous suffering caused by this disaster. More than 2,000 people perished that night, virtually disappearing from the face of the earth. In addition, approximately 30,000 Sea Islanders instantly saw their homes, crops and livelihoods destroyed.

As cries for help poured out, as request for food, blankets, medicines and basic needs were reported in newspapers and magazine, there was very little State and Federal government could (or would) do. There were only private donations of cash, clothes, ancient army tents and inadequate food. Fortunately, for these poor and destitute people, Clara Barton and the American Red Cross arrived and set up a massive relief effort. Ironically, Barton was asked to come and provide support by South Carolina's most notorious and racist governor.

At the end of my quest, researching what is arguably the greatest natural disaster to ever affect South Carolina, and the second deadliest hurricane in US History, it seems obvious that the race of the victims played a part in the lack of disaster relief and aid. What's apparent too, is that those black Sea Islanders, during the era of Jim Crow, were largely ignored, because they were disenfranchised both economically and politically.

The Great Sea Islands Hurricane and Tidal Wave occurred during the worst possible time, at the height of the economic Panic and Depression of 1893. Popular opinions on charity differed too, while there was some outpouring of clothes, food and money, there were many more who felt that too much was done for the Sea Islanders and they should fend for themselves and not be given free rations or money because it would demoralize the people. It was a storm of politics and charity during the Jim Crow era.

As an appendix, I've included a transcript from an interview I produced with Dr. Walter Edgar, noted historian, author, radio personality and professor at the University of South Carolina. Dr. Edgar was gracious enough to offer his expert opinion and knowledge of the time period, politics and the effects of the storm. His insight offers an established historian's point of view. Of which I am very grateful.

Craig G. Metts
18 January 2012

INTRODUCTION:

The State of South Carolina and specifically the coastline along the Atlantic Ocean is very familiar with devastating disasters such as fires, diseases, floods, storms, hurricanes, and even earthquakes (the "Great Earthquake of Charleston" struck the city on the 31st of August 1886 killing more than sixty people).

Sailors Home, Charity of the Charleston Port Society after the Great Earthquake[2]

Certainly of all disasters, hurricanes and the storm surges that they bring are the most costly of natural disasters to affect the South Carolina coastline. Indeed, over one hundred hurricanes and tropical storms have impacted South Carolina since the year

---

[2] Courtesy of the South Caroliniana Library Archives

1600; and since 1900, four hurricanes have made landfall with winds and surges that place them in category three and four on the Saffir Simpson Scale[3]. The precise classifications of earlier storms are difficult to assess, and the study of pre-1900 storms can only be based upon approximate measurements of wind speed, water measurements, and oral accounts. One such pre-1900 hurricane that merits examination was the hurricane and storm surge of the 27th – 28th of August 1893 known as the "Hurricane and Tidal Wave of the Sea Islands off the Coast of South Carolina"[4].

The southern coastline of South Carolina between Charleston and Savannah, Georgia is bordered by a series of small and isolated islands and inlets that are generally known as the Sea Islands. The Sea Islands were the home of many of the state's largest plantations and consequently, the largest populations of slaves. Since colonial times the islands produced crops including vegetables, indigo, rice and especially, a very famous variety of

[3] Storm information was compiled from data listed on the National Oceanic and Atmospheric Administration Home Page, *Hurricane and Tropical Storm Data 1600 – Present… Georgia and South Carolina Storms*. Available from http://wchs.csc.noaa.gov/hurrican.html

[3] Barton, Clara, *The Red Cross in Peace and War*. (Washington, D.C.: American Historical Press, 1904), p. 197.

long staple cotton known as "Sea Island cotton." In the aftermath of the Civil War, large plantations were broken up into smaller farms, inhabited by the newly emancipated slaves and their descendants.

Going to the field, James Hopkins Plantation, Edisto Island, South Carolina[5]

The Sea Islanders eked out a meager existence living in shacks and shanties and by 1893, the population was 40,000 or more. According to *Harper's Weekly*, "Eighty-five per cent of these people are colored; the remaining fifteen per cent include the planters and their agents, the storekeepers, the owners of business

---

[5] Prints and Photographs Division, Library of Congress

plants, and some scattered crackers."[6]

A Typical Sea Islander Cabin 1890s, Port Royal, South Carolina[7]

Except for a hurricane on the 11th of September 1883 and another on the 25th of August 1885, very little damage from natural disasters had befallen the South Carolina coastline since the end of the Civil War. Certainly the Charleston earthquake of 1886 caused great destruction, but the majority of the damage seems to have occurred in the city of Charleston. The state's poor economy was based on agriculture and phosphate mining, while its politicians were coming to grips with a post-Reconstruction slump and "Jim

---

[6] Tillinghast, B. F., "The Present and the Future of the Carolina Sea Islanders." *Harper's Weekly* (9th June 1894), p. 548.

[7] Library of Congress, Special Collections

Crow" laws. The Sea Islands received the crushing blow of the hurricane of the 27th and 28th of August 1893.

The "Great Sea Islands Hurricane and Tidal Wave" was arguably the most costly in damage to property, human life and historical consequence to the state of South Carolina. However, perhaps because of the isolated location and the fact that most of the victims were African-Americans, this severe and deadly storm has never been fully examined or accounted for in the many histories of South Carolina.

THE STORM:

Life on the isolated islands was a simple and austere existence based upon phosphate mining, farming and fishing. The year of 1893 for St. Helena was described as "...a good one in spite of some natural set-backs. Record crops were partly gathered and the people felt more independent and self confident than ever before."[8] All seemed calm before the storm.

Planting Sweet Potatoes, James Hopkins Plantation, Edisto Island, South Carolina[9]

While weather forecasting and measurements were primitive, a storm was being tracked. On the 24th of August 1893

---

[8] Dabbs, Edith M., *Sea Island Diary, A History of St. Helena Island.* (Spartanburg, S.C.: The Reprint company, 1983), p. 195.

[9] Prints and Photographs Division, Library of Congress

the storm was "...sighted far down in the West Indies," and on Friday, the 25th of August, "...storm signals were set." The storm was "sighted" at sea and seemed to be heading towards Florida, and South Carolina received little warning. Certainly, the isolation of the Sea Islands prevented much warning of the storm. But by Saturday the 26th the storm began to move northward so that "...ship-masters were warned to look for rough waters off of the Savannah bar."[10] The storm was originally tracked as it moved away from Havana, Cuba, and the Bahamas from the 24th through 25th of August until it went out to sea by Saturday the 26th. Communication and observation of the storm was difficult if not impossible given the technology of the nineteenth century, so the storm's exact location was unknown as long as it was at sea.[11]

According to data compiled by the National Oceanic and Atmospheric Administration (NOAA), the storm began off the northwestern coast of Africa and moved westward across the Atlantic Ocean.

---

[10]Stovall, Pleasant A., "The Cyclone in the South." *Harper's Weekly* (16th September 1893), p. 882.

[11] Hamilton, Elizabeth Verner, *Storm Center*. (Charleston, South Carolina: Tradd Street Press, 1983.) p. vii

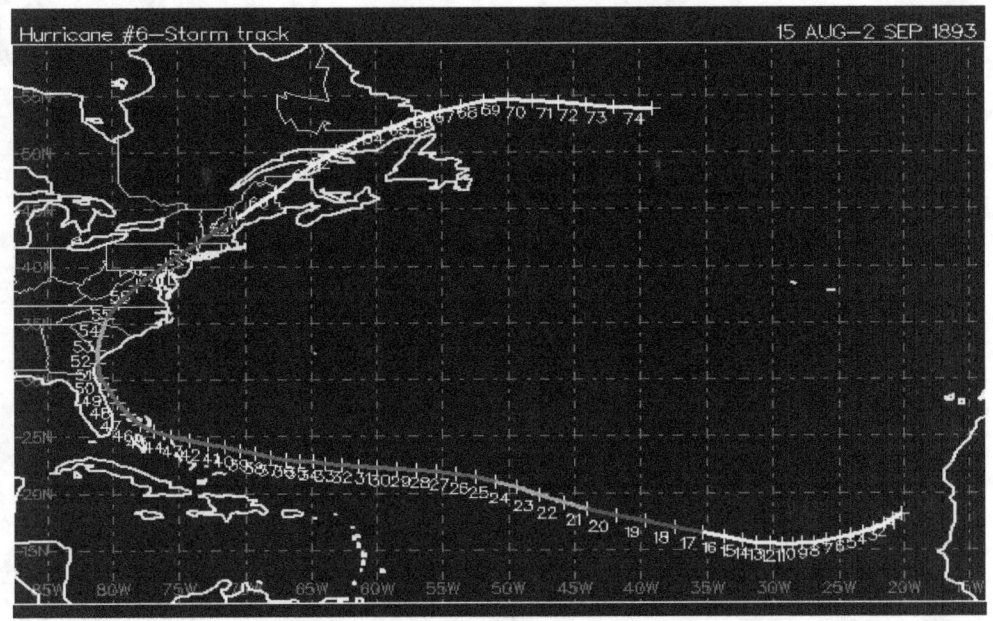

Hurricane No. 6 – Storm Track, 15th August-2nd September 1893[12]

Passing through the Caribbean, it skirted across the Bahamas Islands where it turned north and headed towards the U.S. mainland. The first trajectories indicated that it was moving towards Florida, but the storm stayed at sea and moved along the Florida coastline. The eye passed over Savannah, Georgia in the early morning of the 28th of August 1893.

---

[12] Vietor, Daniel, *Hurricane / Tropical Data, Atlantic Hurricane Tracking Data by Year, Tropical Cyclone Data for 1893*. West Lafayette IN: Dept of Earth & Atmospheric Sciences, Purdue University.

Though the Saffir Simpson Scale had not been developed, NOAA tracking information indicates that the hurricane had developed into a class three hurricane (wind speeds of one hundred miles per hour) somewhere over the mid-Atlantic. The storm's winds maintained the class three statuses until landfall and incredibly maintained hurricane status (wind speeds of sixty five miles per hour or more) until it entered the state of Maine on the 30th of August.[13]

On the Sea Islands, the first effects of the storm were felt when rain began on Sunday, the 20th of August, and continued through the week, keeping most people inside. The isolated islands received little or no warning of the approaching hurricane. "Beaufort people had telegraphic warnings and bulletins of a vicious hurricane moving up the Florida coast.... For isolated St. Helena and other islands without communication there was no warning."[14] For the vast majority of Sea Islanders between Charleston and Beaufort, there was no warning, other than excessive rain. The

---

[13] Vietor, Daniel, *Hurricane / Tropical Data, Atlantic Hurricane Tracking Data by Year, Tropical Cyclone Data for 1893.* West Lafayette IN: Dept of Earth & Atmospheric Sciences, Purdue University (Hurricane No. 6 – Storm Track, 15th August-2nd September 1893).

[14] Dabbs, Edith M., *Sea Island Diary, A History of St. Helena Island*, p. 195.

approximate area affected by the hurricane was between Savannah, Georgia, and Georgetown, South Carolina. However, the majority of damage seems to have been limited to the extreme coastal region from Beaufort to Sullivan's Island.

The first reports came from Sullivan's Island, and were mentioned in Charleston's daily newspaper, *The News and Courier,* in a very short column where it was reported, "about seven o'clock the wind reached a velocity of 125 miles per hour" and "that every foot of Sullivan's Island was under water at midnight Sunday."[15] The reports from Sullivan's Island would become typical of the rest of the outer islands. At Daufuskie Island the storm was remembered as the worst ever to hit the island, having an eighteen to twenty foot storm surge. The high water from the storm surge was the main killer: "...on St. Helena and Lady's Island hundreds of people were drowned, almost entirely Negro, for they had no way to escape..."[16] In Beaufort and St. Helena, Admiral Beardslee described the Sea Islanders living in small cabins and reported that,

---

[15] *The News and Courier* (Charleston, South Carolina) 29th August 1893, p. 2.

[16] Burn, Billie, *An Island Named Daufuskie.* (Spartanburg, S.C.; The Reprint Company, 1991), p. 462.

"...hundreds of those cabins had been swept from the earth, with all they contained... [and]...the surrounding ocean inundated our islands to depths varying from one to ten feet...the average height of the tidal wave above high water, being about seven feet."[17] The waters were so high that many islands were completely submerged. The following extract is typical of many of the stories from the doomed islands:

> The encroaching tidal wave driven by the fierce hurricane continued more and more to submerge the islands. Men, women and children knowing that the sea surrounded them on all sides, groped in vain for higher ground, and many perished in the attempt. Others climbed to the top of their houses, but this was sure death, as their roofs were soon broken up by the angry waves and carried out to sea. Wiser men and women seized their little ones and hastened to the woods fast as possible, through the deep water; those who could climb the trees were comparatively safe, but the raging

---

[17] Barton, Clara, *The Red Cross in Peace and War*, p. 205.

waves tore many little ones from their mother's grasp and carried them beyond their reach…[18]

Left by the Tide an Illustration depicting a Victim by Drowning[19]

Many of the accounts call the excessively high waters caused by the storm surge of the Sea Islands Hurricane a tidal wave. While tidal waves are generally thought of as a Pacific Ocean phenomenon caused by volcanic and seismic activity, the

---

[18] Mather, Mrs. R. C., *The Storm Swept Coast of South Carolina.* (Woonsocket, R.I.: C. E. Cook, printer, 1894), p. 13.

[19] Harris, Joel Chandler, "The Sea Island Hurricanes, The Devastation." *Scribner's Magazine* (February 1894), p. 236.

sheer size of the storm surge caused by this hurricane must have been frightening. A contributing factor in the extreme heights of the storm surge from the August 1893 hurricane was that this storm made landfall during high tide and produced the highest storm tides on record for the South Carolina coastline. The highest tides were in Savannah and estimated from between 17.0 feet to 19.5 feet above MSL (Mean Sea Level). At Charleston the high tide was measured at 8.5 feet above MSL and at Edisto Island a high tide of 10.9 feet above MSL was attained (the normal high tide for Edisto averages 6.0 feet above MSL).[20] Beaufort and St. Helena's Island would have had high tides somewhere between those of Savannah and Edisto. These extremely high storm tides coupled with the severe wind and storm surge of the hurricane could have caused the surface of the ocean to rise well over twenty to twenty-five feet above normal sea level, easily covering many of the low lying Sea Islands.

---

[20] Myers, Vance A., *Storm Tide Frequencies on the South Carolina Coast*; NOAA Technical Report NWS-1. Office of Hydrology. (Silver Spring, Maryland; National Oceanic and Atmospheric Administration, June 1975). Information compiled from page 22, page 74 and Table A-1 (Frequency analysis of hurricane tidal elevations affecting Charleston, S.C., 1893 – 1964).

THE AFTERMATH:

The destruction of the Sea Islands was not known until days later. Charleston's *The News and Courier* first reported the, "…record of terror and ruin wrought by the great disaster of 1885 remains the greatest natural disaster in the city's history…"[21] The preliminary measurements of wind and first damage reports seemed minimal, with only slight damage to houses, trees, piers and a few ships.

However, the following day's newspaper recanted, saying that, "…the account of the Cyclone published in *The News and Courier* still left half the story of the disaster untold, Charleston was a city in ruins."[22]

With only a day to comprehend the damage in Charleston, the newspaper on the 29th of August reported three people dead in Charleston, and three on Sullivan's Island. Similarly, the Columbia daily newspaper, *The State,* reported on 29 August, "Although the

---

[21] *The News and Courier*, 28th August 1893, p. 1.

[22] *The News and Courier*, 29th August 1893, p. 1.

damage to property was immense, no casualties to citizens reported."[23]

The fierce storm that hit Charleston and the Sea Islands was later remembered as "...worse than the one of 1885; the wind was actually recorded at 120 miles per hour."[24]

After the Storm - East Battery, Looking Northeast, Charleston, South Carolina[25]

[23] *The State* (Columbia, South Carolina), 29th August 1893, p. 1.

[24] Mulloy, Robert, *Charleston, A Gracious Heritage.* (New York & London; D. Appleton-Century Company, Inc., [date unknown]), p. 271.

[25] *Harper's Weekly*, "The Public Interest in disasters" (16th September 1893), Page 882

After the Storm – Atlantic Wharves, Charleston, South Carolina[26]

Later reports from Charleston were of severe property damage, including downed power and telegraph lines that left the city out of communication with the outside world. While the damage to Charleston was severe, it was minor in comparison to that wrought against the outer islands. For the next three days after the storm, the news grew worse, until it was realized how devastating the storm was. The hardest hit area seemed to be Beaufort and the Islands of Daufuskie, Hilton Head, St. Helena,

---

[26] *Harper's Weekly*, "The Public Interest in disasters" (16th September 1893), Page 882

Fripp, Hunting, Lady, Edisto, and Kiawah. The boundaries lay between Savannah to the south and Charleston to the north.

After the Storm – A House in Beaufort, South Carolina[27]

Slowly the reports came in of the death toll. First a scattered handful was reported, then the number grew into several hundred and later the losses of life reached the thousands. Of the deaths, *The State* reported that "…fifteen dead bodies were found in one house," "…bodies strewn through beach and marsh," and added that "When the dead bodies are found the survivors of the disaster just dig a shallow hole in the marsh and dump them in it." On 3rd

[27] Prints and Photographs Division, Library of Congress

September, one week after the storm had struck the coastline, the new death toll estimates were from one thousand to one thousand five hundred.[28]

The storm garnered national and international coverage. *The New York Times* carried the story until the 3rd of September. The *Times* estimated that the total cost for damages was "Over ten million dollars worth of property destroyed."[29] The newspaper expressed a national concern for the hurricane sufferers, trying to raise money and awareness of the suffering. The Sea Islands Hurricane received a week's worth of coverage in London's *The Times*. A report of the destruction was given for Sullivan's Island along with a description of the hurricane: "The New Brighton Hotel, the finest establishment of the kind on the island, is said to be a total wreck. It was in the path of the 'tornado,' and it is rumored that many persons in the island have perished."[30]

---

[28] *The State*, 3rd August 1893, p. 1.

[29] *The New York Times*, 29th August 1893, p. 1.

[30] *The Times* (London) 31st August 1893, p. 3. (It is likely that the term 'tornado' was used to describe the hurricane.)

The landscape of the Sea Islands was often described as looking as though war had ravished the land. Mrs. R.C. Mather, in her book *The Storm Swept Coast of South Carolina,* paints this account:

> When the morning dawned, lo, the fruitful field, ripe for harvest had become desert waste. Immense heaps of sedge were piled high far inland; the shores were thickly strewn with wrecked vessels, household goods and dead animals far as the eye could reach in all directions. Fruit and forest trees lay prostrate. Death and destruction reigned triumphant all around. Bridges were down, railroads torn up, telegraph lines destroyed, so no mail could come through. Highways too, were so obstructed by fallen trees that communication between settlements on the same island was very difficult.[31]

---

[31] Mather, Mrs. R. C., *The Storm Swept Coast of South Carolina*, p. 37.

An illustration Depicting the Wreck of *The City of Savannah*[32]

Tales of the property damage and wrecked and lost ships filled the newspapers, almost as much as the reports of the death toll and homeless. The great passenger steamer *The City of Savannah* was feared lost at sea, but its wreckage was found off the Coast of Hunting Island. The entire crew and passengers weathered the storm by lashing themselves to the rigging for three days without water or food. One of the passengers, John MacDonald on his way from Boston to Savannah for business, read of the relief effort after he was rescued and taken to Savannah. He

[32] Harris, Joel Chandler, "The Sea Island Hurricanes, The Devastation." *Scribner's Magazine* (February 1894), p. 239.

was so moved that he gave up his business plans and volunteered to work for the Red Cross relief program. During the relief effort, MacDonald even married a trained Red Cross nurse from Milwaukee, Ida Battell.[33] Another such ship, The *Yemassee* was also feared lost, but survived by sailing into the mid-Atlantic and escaping the storm, arriving in Charleston on the 31st of August with very little damage. Many ships were picked up and carried overland, demonstrating the great power and force of the storm. *Harper's Weekly* gives one such account: "A schooner passed over Tybee, and dragged with its anchor several hundred yards of railroad track into the woods. Steel rails were wrapped like hairpins around giant oaks."[34]

The destruction reached inland as well, for the hurricane traveled from Savannah to Columbia and on northward through the eastern United States along the Atlantic seaboard. Heavy rains and winds ravaged both eastern Georgia and the majority of South Carolina, with damages as far north as Charlotte, North Carolina.

---

[33] Barton, Clara, *The Red Cross, In Peace and War*, p. 211.

[34] Stovall, Pleasant A., "The Cyclone in the South", Harper's Weekly, p. 882.

In the interior of South Carolina the newspapers reported similar stories of strong winds blowing down houses, trees and telegraph lines, with large scale agricultural damage from Darlington, Bishopville, Timmonsville, Sumter, Allendale and Horry. Only a few deaths were reported along with several minor injuries and losses of livestock. The phosphate industry from mainland locations in Darlington County to factories in the low country seemed to have suffered very heavy losses with some factories being completely destroyed.[35]

As time went on the estimates of the total number of dead and homeless varied greatly. Edith M. Dabbs in a *Sea Island Diary* reports that "...some three thousand of them who drowned, it was. Another twenty to thirty thousand, over mainland and islands together, were left homeless with no means of subsistence..."[36] In *The Storm Swept Coast of South Carolina*, by Mrs. R.C. Mather, the estimate is much lower. "Over a thousand men, women and children perished, over twenty thousand it is estimated escaped

---

[35] *The State*, 31 August 1893, p. 5.

[36] Dabbs, Edith M., *Sea Island Diary, A History of St. Helena Island*, p. 196.

with their lives only, and seventy thousand, it is said, on the islands and low shores of the mainland, lost their crops."[37]

The final death-toll fell between one and three thousand people, depending upon the sources. The exact number is and was then, impossible to tell. Bodies were found weeks later, and often quickly counted and buried in mass graves on the spot. It is impossible to tell how many uncounted souls were washed out to sea, given the isolation and the rough census figures. By the best estimates the death toll is likely to be around two thousand.

In a NOAA technical memorandum titled *The Deadliest Atlantic cyclones, 1492 – Present,* the Sea Islands Hurricane with two thousand deaths ranks as the 20th deadliest since 1492. Indeed, based upon the numbers of storm fatalities since 1492, the hurricane was the deadliest ever to hit the Atlantic Seaboard, and the second deadliest ever to hit the United States.

---

[37] Mather, Mrs. R. C., *The Storm Swept Coast of South Carolina*, pp. 11 & 12.

Only the Galveston, Texas, hurricane on the 8th of
September 1900 with eight thousand or more storm fatalities was
worse.[38]

---

[38] Rappaport, Edward N. & Fernandez-Partagas, Jose, *The Deadliest Atlantic Tropical Cyclones,*
   1492 – Present. (Washington, D.C.: NOAA Technical Memorandum, NWS NHC 47, January
   1995). Information was compiled from charts and tables from this source.

THE RELIEF EFFORT:

By the beginning of September the newspapers were reporting large-scale famine and the number of deaths due to the storm was increasing. Early accounts put the death toll at six hundred in Beaufort and Port Royal alone. The first appeal was made by a Col. J. H. Averill, a receiver for the railroad, from Yemasee, South Carolina on the 31st of August, who reported six hundred dead and seven thousand homeless in and around Beaufort.

Governor Benjamin R. (Pitchfork Ben) Tillman[39]

---

[39] Prints and Photographs Division, Library of Congress.

Having just returned from visiting the Chicago World's Fair on the 31st of August, Governor Benjamin R. (Pitchfork Ben) Tillman responded by presenting an executive proclamation to the public and newspapers calling for public help and contributions for the sufferers. Tillman emphasized that, "The fact that these are poor colored farmers, whose homes have been ruined and crops destroyed, appeals with peculiar force to every right-thinking person." He then went a step further by establishing a relief fund and setting up a relief committee of seven persons, with at least two of the members to be black. The Governor also appointed Dr. J. W. Babcock as his representative to investigate the disaster scene and return with a first hand account. [40]

The State reported the next day that nearly six hundred dollars had been raised with Governor Tillman contributing to the first effort. Residents of Charleston collected over one thousand five hundred dollars in goods and money. Senator M.C. Butler of South Carolina secured an agreement with the Secretary of the Army for tents for the homeless and asked for support and relief

---

[40] *The State*, 1st September 1893, p. 1.

from the Secretary of the Navy. President Grover Cleveland gave his moral support and approval for the Army to send in three hundred tents requested by Senator Butler.[41]

Other support from the federal government was called for. On the 4th of September, the South Carolina delegation of Congressmen met and drafted a joint resolution asking Congress for an appropriation of two hundred thousand dollars. The resolution was to be presented to Congress during the following week.[42] However, national relief did not look promising due to the severe economic depression of that year and the political struggles over the tariff and silver issues.

---

[41] *The News and Courier,* 6th September 1893, p. 1.

[42] *The State, 5th* September 1893, p. 1

President Grover Cleveland's Inauguration in 1893[43]

Private aid came from all over. From New York on 5 September a total of one thousand three hundred dollars and other help were donated. Other contributions in money and goods were received from Brooklyn, Boston, Jacksonville, Philadelphia, and Washington. Groups sent supplies of goods such as clothes, lumber, food, seed and tools. The donated relief materials and money were sent daily to the state relief committee in Beaufort. By the end of the first week of the relief effort the sum amassed was nearly ten thousand dollars. [44]

---

[43] Prints and Photographs Division, Library of Congress

By the end of the first week in September though, it was clear that the death toll was indeed over one thousand five hundred, and that the great numbers of homeless and impoverished peoples were not exaggerated. The preliminary report telegraphed to the Governor by Dr. Babcock revealed a great deal of property loss in Beaufort and St. Helena Island and especially "Diarrhoea (sic) and malaria fever caused by drinking brackish water and exposure and sickening stench from dead bodies."[45] Furthermore, upon returning to Columbia, Dr. Babcock reported personally to Governor Tillman that the destruction of life and property was much greater than had been thought, "...over 20,000 people, survivors of the recent disastrous hurricane work, were staring starvation and pestilence in the face..."[46] Most accounts of those in need place the numbers from twenty thousand to thirty thousand homeless and starving. *Harper's Weekly* in June of 1894, after the numbers had been assessed, reported, "Of the 40,000 islanders it was determined that three out of four must have

[44] Relief totals compiled from *The State,* 3rd & 8th September 1893; and *The News and Courier,* 6th, 7th & 8th September 1893.

[45] *The State,* 6th September 1893, p. 1.

[46] *The State,* 8th September 1893, p. 1.

some sort of assistance."[47]   Therefore, thirty thousand seems the best estimate of those severely affected by the hurricane.

Realizing that the money and relief efforts being raised were too meager compared to the enormous numbers of disaster victims, both Tillman and Babcock publicly pleaded for help from the nation. However, 1893 found the national economy in the greatest depression of the nineteenth century. The national economy and political climate were in a state of despair, and little help was forthcoming.

Congressman George W. Murray[48]

[47] Tillinghast, B. F., "The Present and the Future of the Carolina Sea Islanders," Harper's Weekly, p. 548.

South Carolina Congressman George W. Murray (an African-American) was one of the Congressmen who proposed the joint resolution. Realizing that no appropriation was possible, he gave up and instead prepared a bill asking for one hundred and fifty thousand rations to be distributed by the War Department.[49] Governor Tillman, Senator Butler and the Beaufort relief committee began to look for alternate solutions.

---

[48] Culp, D.W., ed. Twentieth Century Negro Literature.

[49] *The State,* 8th September 1893, p. 1.

THE RED CROSS:

President of the American Red Cross - Clara Barton[50]

Shortly After Governor Tillman's second appeal for relief on Friday, the 8th of September 1893, this one "To The People of the United States,"[51] a series of telegrams concerning the American Red Cross were sent between the President of the Red Cross, Clara Barton, Senator Butler and Governor Tillman. The American Red Cross was interested in lending relief assistance. The whole

---

[50] Prints and Photographs Division, Library of Congress.

[51] *The State,* 8th September 1893, p. 1.

affair seems to have begun from an offhanded remark that the Governor made after hearing that the death toll had reached over one thousand. *The State* reported on the 3rd of September that while the governor was pacing up and down his office he wondered out loud, "…if in this calamity it will be of any use to get the Red Cross Society to send its representatives there." The governor went on to say that the relief effort should not be so much a charitable one, but one that provided support for the people to get back to their way of life. Furthermore, he made an appeal that people not send money, but purchase provisions and food for the victims. [52]

On the 8th of September Clara Barton telegraphed Governor Tillman offering to send a representative to the Sea Islands to assess if there were a need for the Red Cross. Barton sent the telegram after speaking to Senator Butler in Washington, receiving his support to involve the Red Cross. Governor Tillman, who promptly rejected the Red Cross' aid, seems to have misunderstood the telegram because it came directly from Clara Barton with no mention of the Red Cross. The next day, on

---

[52] *The State,* 3rd September 1893, p. 1.

Saturday the 9th, Barton wired again to explain that she had contacted Tillman as a representative of the Red Cross. Other Red Cross representatives, Doctor Joseph Gardner and George H. Pullman, telegraphed as well to affirm the seriousness of Barton's offer. Governor Tillman's second telegram accepted Barton's offer, with the warning:

> While contributions are liberal, the work of relief here will be heavy and long continued, and I fear means of relief will prove inadequate, I therefore ask you to assist in any way you think best.[53]

On Friday, the 15th of September Clara Barton and her entourage accompanied by Senator Butler, made their way by train to meet Governor Tillman in Beaufort where they were to tour the disaster area. Barton told *The State,* "…that her society was not coming here to take control of the relief work, as had been stated, but was coming down to do Red Cross work…"[54] Barton seems to have feared that the Red Cross was not taken seriously. She

---

[53] *The State,* 12th September 1893, p. 8.

[54] *The State,* 16th September 1893, p. 4.

stressed that it was not a charity giving handouts, but rather a support agency that provided assistance to people to get back on their feet after disaster. The Red Cross had already assisted in disaster relief to flood and famine victims, as well as providing assistance to Charleston during the earthquake of 1886.

A conference was called on the 18th of September in Charleston of the Beaufort relief committee, Governor Tillman, Senator Butler, Clara Barton and the other representatives of the Red Cross. The general state of the hurricane victims was discussed and general estimates were made of the relief that would be needed. After the discussion the Red Cross was formally asked to assume charge over the relief effort. Governor Tillman made the request to send all aid contributions to the Red Cross for distribution and proposed that the Beaufort relief committee be dissolved in favor of the Red Cross. Facing the challenge of a long-term relief effort, the Red Cross set-up its headquarters in Beaufort.[55]

---

[55] *The State,* 19th September 1893, p. 1.

A somewhat different picture of the situation was painted by Clara Barton in her 1904 account of the Red Cross entitled, *The Red Cross, In Peace and War.* Barton was familiar with the geography of the South Carolina Sea Islands, because of her many months of war relief effort during the siege of Charleston in 1863 – 64. After hearing about the devastating hurricane and storm surge she says that she feared the worst:

> I thought I saw no escape for the inhabitants and that all must have perished; and so replied to all inquirers at first made as to whether this were not a disaster for the Red Cross to relieve, 'No, there was nothing left to relieve.'[56]

Once the reports came in that there were tens of thousands of destitute survivors, Barton then feared that the relief effort would be too great for the meager resources of the Red Cross, and urged that the State of South Carolina or the Federal government must assist. However, once she realized that South Carolina was too poor a state to provide aid and that because of the severe depression of the United States economy, and the Federal

---

[56] Barton, Clara, *The Red Cross, In Peace and War*, p. 201.

Government was going to do very little, she approached Senator Butler. Barton writes that Butler "...dropped all business, telegraphed at once to Governor Tillman at Columbia to learn of the conditions and urgently requested us to go..."[57]

Barton remained in Beaufort, where at first the Red Cross worked with the Beaufort relief commission until the society could study the situation at first hand. More than a month after the disaster, on the 1st of October, the duties of the Beaufort relief commission were surrendered to the Red Cross. At the request of the Red Cross, the members of the Beaufort committee continued to serve as an advisory board. The great task of the Red Cross was best described by Clara Barton's biographer Elizabeth Brown Pryor:

> From the beginning it had been evident that this would be prolonged work, for it was necessary to provide for the people until their next crop could be harvested, nearly a year later. Thirty thousand people and thirty thousand dollars meant there would be only one dollar per year per person.[58]

[57] Barton, Clara, *The Red Cross, In Peace and War*, p. 201.

The Red Cross set about to feed, clothe, and assist in rebuilding the homes and farms lost to the storm. It mobilized and set up a number of "districts" with district leaders in charge of rationing out available supplies. There were nineteen districts total, and all reported to Clara Barton at the Beaufort headquarters.

Red Cross Workers Sorting Potatoes, Beaufort, South Carolina[59]

The Red Cross set a standard ration for a family of seven at "...a half a peck of grits a week and a pound of pork..."[60] Those

[58] Pryor, Elizabeth Brown, *Clara Barton, Professional Angel.* (Philadelphia: University of Pennsylvania Press, 1987), p. 276.

[59] Prints and Photographs Division, Library of Congress

[60] Barton, Clara, *The Red Cross, In Peace and War*, p. 237.

who were sick received coffee, tea, beef broth and extra rations. Laborers were given double portions at day's end for work that included / the repair and re-building of houses, the digging of ditches for flood protection, the clearing out of wells and digging new ones and the odd jobs necessary for the relief effort. The organization proved very efficient with very limited resources. "To prepare for planting, nearly three hundred miles of drainage ditches were dug... (and) One million feet of lumber went into construction of new houses."[61]

Laborers on Ration Day for St. Helena and Ladies Island, South Carolina[62]

---

[61] Pryor, Elizabeth Brown, *Clara Barton, Professional Angel*, p. 277.

While the Red Cross put men to work as laborers to rebuild the storm ravaged farms on the Sea Islands, the women who were not farming were recruited into sewing "circles" to repair, mend and make clothing, blankets, bedding and other cloth goods. In the Hilton Head district alone "...3,400 garments were repaired and given away..."[63] Some clothing donated was handed out as is and was apparently last season's Victorian fashion.

Red Cross Clothing-Room[64]

---

[62] Tillinghast, B. F., "The Present and the Future of the Carolina Sea Islanders," Harper's Weekly, p. 548

[63] Barton, Clara, *The Red Cross, In Peace and War*, p. 221.

[64] Tillinghast, B. F., "The Present and the Future of the Carolina Sea Islanders," Harper's Weekly,

The State newspaper made these comments (excerpted from a history on the Red Cross):

Never was there such a revival in sartorial styles. It was common spectacle to see rice-field hands, black Negro women, who had never worn anything costing more than 'ten cents a yard,' plumed in velvets and silk and crowned with last year's fashionable millinery creations, all contributed from the wardrobes of Northern subscribers to the relief supplies.[65]

In addition to the practical relief of food, clothing and shelter, the Red Cross provided health care and some meager forms of education to the Sea Islands population. It was estimated that the average clinic treated about seventy-three people a day. These figures do not include those treated by travelling doctors. "At the end of the Sea Islands' relief, boasted Barton, not one death from illness was recorded."[66] Those traveling and distributing aid were

---

p. 548

[65] Dulles, Foster Rhea, *The American Red Cross, A History*. (New York: Harper & Brothers Publishers, 1950), p. 32.

[66] Pryor, Elizabeth Brown, *Clara Barton, Professional Angel*, p. 278.

instructed to give the Sea Islanders a "good practical talk" that would include the following subjects: *Owe no man anything*; *How to keep out of debt*; *Don't sell cotton before it is picked*; *Plant more vegetables, and why*; and *Divide cottages into rooms*"[67].

Reports indicate that the people of the Sea Islands cooperated and appeared to have a better standard of living after the Red Cross left in June of 1894. Clara Barton was seen as the figurehead of the Red Cross and thereby held in some reverence. "... the name 'Miss Cla' Ba'ton' was on everybody's tongue, the infant girls named Clara Barton and the boys 'Red Cross'..."[68]

---

[67] Barton, Clara, *The Red Cross, In Peace and War*, p. 231.
[68] Ibid., p. 216.

POLITICS AND PUBLIC OPINION:

The Red Cross closed its doors in June 1894, "...feeling that if it stayed longer the Sea Islanders would become too dependent, health conditions were greatly improved, homes largely restored, and a fine cotton crop was in prospect."[69] There seemed to have been a great deal of public curiosity regarding the Red Cross' relief efforts.

Joel Chandler Harris[70]

---

[69] Dulles, Foster Rhea, *The American Red Cross, A History*, p. 33.

[70] Prints and Photographs Division, Library of Congress

Scribner's Magazine sent Joel Chandler Harris, author of the "Uncle Remus" and "Br'er Rabbit" stories off to the Sea Islands to investigate and report on the efforts of the Red Cross. An excerpt of Harris' article follows:

> I went to the Sea Islands with no prejudice against the Red Cross Society, but certainly with no prepossession in its favor. I had pictured it in my mind as a sort of fussy and contentious affair... As a matter of fact, the Red Cross Society as I saw it at Beaufort is something entirely different... There are no exhibitions of self-importance... There is no display – no tortuous cross-examination of applicants – no needless delay.[71]

The State on the 18th of October 1893 published an article entitled "Work of the Red Cross, Miss Clara Barton's Wonderful Story." The Columbia newspaper presented Barton and the American Red Cross in a very favorable light, arguing that the relief effort "...implies the housing, feeding, clothing, and nursing of

---

[71] Harris, Joel Chandler, "The Sea Island Hurricanes, The Devastation." *Scribner's Magazine* (February 1894), p. 247.

30,000 people for eight months with no aid from the government and no funds but direct charity from the American people."[72]

The Red Cross' relief efforts did have its critics. In the *Review of Reviews*, author Sophia Wells Royce Williams praised Barton and the Red Cross but noted that the relief work,

> ...has met criticism in some well-informed quarters... and ...when one asks for detailed reports, for itemized statements of disbursements, for careful recapitulation of its labors, its achievements, its failures, its experience and the teaching and lesson of its work – these things either do not exist or are not furnished.[73]

The national controversy seems to have arisen from the Red Cross' relief effort at Johnstown, Pennsylvania after the 1st of June 1889. A dam burst above the city of thirty thousand, and the flooding waters killed over two thousand people. The Johnstown Flood Relief Commission gave out one million, six hundred

---

[72] *The State*, 18th October 1893, p. 2.

[73] Williams, Sophia Wells Royce, "Miss Clara Barton and the Red Cross, A Study of Relief Work and of Agencies to Meet the Suffering from War, Pestilence and Catastrophe." *The Review of Reviews* (March 1894), pp. 314 & 315.

thousand dollars in support and the Red Cross over the course of five months "...distributed relief in kind estimated at a value of $200,000 and $39,000 in cash, including for the first time salaries for clerical workers... There was, however, a strange echo that was to arise in later years to haunt Miss Barton and her reputation."[74] Her biographer admits that Barton lacked accounting and money skills, and that lack became a serious problem. "What had started as small in-house gripes about the lack of reports... had grown into loud and public protest."[75]

In early May 1894 a controversy also arose in South Carolina as a result of a letter of appeal written by Thomas R. Heyward calling for additional relief efforts. Heyward, a Bluffton resident, represented a group of white farmers that the Red Cross had allegedly not helped. The letter was sent to major newspapers in and out of state as well as to Governor Tillman. Heyward accused Barton and the Red Cross of ignoring a group of 600 poor farmers who were also victims of the hurricane. He took advantage

[74] Hurd, Charles, and Illustrations by Gil Walker, *The Compact History of the American Red Cross.* (New York: Hawthorn Books, Inc.) pp. 68 & 69.

[75] Pryor, Elizabeth Brown, *Clara Barton, Professional Angel*, p. 280.

of the public criticism about the "mismanagement" of relief funds by the Red Cross. Heyward stated, "...the Red Cross authorities had disgracefully misused their authority and that they were more than partisan in the distribution of the charity." "...that the white citizens of this community have not, up to date, received $300 in supplies, while thousands have been issued out to Negroes."[76] Oddly, in the same newspaper and on the same page, there is an article reporting that Sarah R. Keyser of Philadelphia had presented a silk Red Cross banner to Governor Tillman, who graciously accepted it for the Red Cross and the good deeds that they had performed. Subsequently, *The State* for the next two days began to demonize the Red Cross over the whole "Bluffton controversy," reacting to the rumors of Barton's poor bookkeeping and mismanagement.

Upon hearing the criticism over the "Bluffton controversy," Clara Barton "...was shocked and hurt at the unfair reports... and she misguidedly (sic) tried to answer each accusation with detailed reports of the work."[77] Barton fired off an open letter to the people

[76] *The State,* 18th May 1894, p. 4.

[77] Pryor, Elizabeth Brown, *Clara Barton, Professional Angel*, p. 280.

of South Carolina and the Bluffton farmers in *The News and Courier* on 1 June.[78] In the letter, Barton declared that she had specifically addressed the issue of mainland hurricane victims like the Bluffton farmers in a letter to Governor Tillman the previous December. The letter stated that the Red Cross could only help those in the most need, those being the Sea Islanders, and that the State legislature should step in to assist the smaller number of mainland storm victims.

Barton publicly blamed the governor for not taking action. She felt that "...Governor Tillman, who had begged her to come to South Carolina in the first place, [had begun] to use the organization's troubles for his own political ends."[79] However, Governor Tillman had indeed acted on Barton's December letter. In a proclamation dated the 18th of December 1893, the Governor informed the General Assembly that he had received a letter from Clara Barton that spoke of her concern about the lack of resources for the inland hurricane victims. Tillman voiced concern for inland

[78] *The News and Courier,* 1st June 1894, p. 1.

[79] Pryor, Elizabeth Brown, *Clara Barton, Professional Angel*, p. 280.

farmers in Colleton County and St. Helena and asked for appropriations. Tillman went even further, "Having failed to adopt my suggestion of having a special committee to investigate the matter, you will have to rely on such information as can be furnished by the representatives in your bodies from the devastated district, to help you."[80] On the 2nd of June 1894, *The State* changed its viewpoint over the "Bluffton controversy" and in a very small one inch column on page four wrote the following:

> The State has two or three times referred briefly to the apparent neglect by the Red Cross of the cyclone sufferers on the mainland and among the whites. It did not say much, for it was waiting for an explanation. The local Refawm (sic) organ, however, has been diligently working up sentiment against the Red Cross, only to discover that the blame for the destitution at Bluffton rest directly upon the Refawm (sic) Legislature, which ignored Governor Tillman's recommendation to appoint a committee of investigation and

---

[80] Tillman, Benjamin R., Governor (1890-1894), *Executive Proclamations; 1890 – 1894*. Special Collections and Manuscripts, South Carolina Department of Archives and History, Columbia, S.C.; call number S526003, p. 181.

his further recommendation of an appropriation for the specific purpose of relieving the suffering on the mainland.[81]

It is still unclear as to why *The State* took so long in getting their facts straight over the controversy. However, the newspaper constantly tried to demonize Governor Tillman who had originally asked for the Red Cross' assistance. By revealing the 'full' story, Governor Tillman and Clara Barton were cleared of the charges of overlooking the Bluffton farmers.

Barton also attempted to clear her name and that of the Red Cross in a letter to *The News and Courier* that followed the Bluffton explanation. The letter pointed out the good work of the Red Cross and praised the citizens of South Carolina for their help.[82] Nevertheless, even after the Red Cross had left the State and returned to Washington, there were still dissenters. Thomas R. Heyward, the Bluffton farmer who opened the controversy, wrote another letter to *The State* on the 23rd of July 1894. Still trying to discredit the Red Cross, Heyward ranted, raved and dismissed

---

[81] *The State,* 2nd June 1894, p. 4.

[82] *The News and Courier,* 23rd June 1894, p. 5.

everything that Clara Barton had said in her June letters printed in *The News and Courier*.[83] It is unknown if Heyward's letters had any lasting effect on South Carolina and the public opinion of Tillman and the Red Cross. Nonetheless, the Red Cross under Clara Barton continued to be plagued by in-fighting and public ridicule on the national level.

One of the great sore spots for the Red Cross and indeed for Governor Tillman, Senator Butler and Congressman Murray, was the lack of aid from the Federal Government. It seemed that Congress "...had generously given aid during the Mississippi and the Ohio floods of 1884,"[84] but now denied it to South Carolina despite several attempts made by State Congressmen. On the 5th of September 1893, Senator Butler presented to the United States Senate a "...petition of Thomas D. Richardson and others, representing the people of Beaufort, S.C. for federal aid and relief for the sufferers by the late cyclone; which was referred to the Committee on Appropriations."[85] As was mentioned previously,

[83] *The State,* 23rd July 1894, p. 6.

[84] Pryor, Elizabeth Brown, *Clara Barton, Professional Angel*, p. 275.

[85] Congressional Record: Containing The Proceedings and Debates of the Fifty-Third Congress,

Congressman Murray, a representative of Beaufort County, who was also a Black Sea Islander, introduced a request for an appropriation of two hundred thousand dollars in a joint resolution on the 11th of September 1893. When the joint resolution was read and was to be voted on, Congressman Constantine Buckley Kilgore, Democrat from Texas, objected to the resolution and a motion was made to refer it to the Committee on Appropriations.[86] Congressman Murray also submitted a joint resolution, (H. Res 39) to secure rations and medicines from the Secretary of War. This bill was also buried in the Committee on Appropriations.[87]

On the 1st of November 1893 Senator George Hoar, Republican from Massachusetts, introduced the last attempt at a federal relief appropriation. Hoar presented a bill (S. 1149) to the United States Senate, requesting an appropriation of fifty thousand dollars; the bill was supported with a memorial from Clara Barton. Hoar presented the bill saying he had "...not the slightest personal

---

first Session. Also, Special Session of the Senate, Volume XXV (Washington; Government Printing Office, 1893), p. 1208.

[86] Ibid., p. 1392.

[87] Ibid., p. 1396.

interest," but because Barton was "...a near neighbor" of his. A bit of party politics ensued, when Senator David Turpie, Democrat from Indiana, immediately objected to it even being read for the first time. Senator Hoar then read the bill himself from the floor over the objections of Turpie. When it came time for the Memorial to be read which needed unanimous consent, Senator Butler from South Carolina, a Democrat, interjected his support and his fellow Democrat, Senator Turpie, withdrew his objections. Barton's Memorial was read but was objected to again. This time it was denounced by Senator William Alfred Peffer from Kansas, a Populist. The Senator stated that if the issue was pressed, he would "...ask that the area be enlarged to take in the whole country... an appropriation sufficiently large be made to set all the idle men in the United States to work."[88]

No bills of relief were approved, and in all the cases the bills were sent to the Committee on Appropriations. There seem to be a number of reasons for this. First, the great problem with most Congressional debate was simply partisan politics. The very

_____

[88] Ibid., p. 3037 – 3039.

capable Congressman Murray always seemed to be opposed by Democrats and the Republican Senator Hoar found his bill and memorial immediately objected to by Senator Turpie, a Democrat. Even after Senator Butler gave the bill his support, Populist Senator Peffer put down the measure. The second reason for the lack of Congressional support seems to have been based upon the poor conditions of the United States economy and the serious depression that had begun that year. Finally, there seems to have been those who cared little for the hurricane victims, the majority of whom were poor Black farmers situated on an isolated group of islands along the South Carolina Coast.

Philadelphian Joseph S. Elkinton who was on his way to Beaufort, observed the damage caused by the hurricane and the relief effort of the Red Cross. Elkinton noted in his Diary that he visited the Red Cross' field office in Beaufort where he took up the issue over the lack of support from Congress. He was told "...that they did not want free rations to be issued, for that it would pauperize and demoralize the people." Elkinton thought that perhaps the declining by Congress to grant appropriation was in part due to the fact that the silver bill and tariff bill "...so wholly engrossed their attention." However, sympathetic to the Red Cross' plight, he went on to say: "There may have been some foundation in what is reported hereaway (sic) that Southern Democrats thought, as did their representatives in Congress, that there were too many "niggers" and it would be well to let them die."[89]

[89] Elkinton, Joseph S., *Selections from the diary and Correspondence of Joseph S. Elkinton, 1830 – 1905*. (Philadelphia: Press of The Leeds & Biddle Co., 1913.) p. 304.

ECONOMY:

Political Cartoon on the Panic and Depression of 1893[90]

The Economic Depression of 1893 and the poor economy of the United States and South Carolina arguably had a large part in the refusal of relief for the disaster victims. It must have been disheartening to Clara Barton and the Red Cross, for just two years earlier, the society has been called in to give relief to flood victims in the Johnstown flood of the 1st of June 1889. The numbers of disaster victims were strikingly similar in the two cases. A little over

---

[90] Courtesy of the University of Missouri Archives

two thousand people died, and the number of persons living in the community that needed assistance was around thirty thousand. The difference was that the Johnsontown Flood Relief Commission and the Red Cross gave out one million, six hundred thousand dollars in support, over fifty-three times more than the thirty thousand dollars raised by donations for the of relief for the Sea Islands.[91] Relief for the Charleston earthquake of 1886, for which the American Red Cross provided some assistance, took place over a similar period of time as the Sea Islands case. The earthquake struck on the 31st of August 1886, and relief was provided until the 25th of July 1887. However, the amount of relief provided totaled almost six hundred thousand dollars.[92] By contrast the American Red Cross provided disaster relief for thirty thousand people in the Sea Islands with only thirty thousand dollars for a period of ten months.

---

[91] Figures were taken from: Hurd, Charles (with Illustrations by Walker, Gil), *The Compact History of the American Red Cross*. (New York: Hawthorn Books, Inc., March 1959), p. 68 & 69.

[92] Charleston City Council, *The Earthquake, 1886; Exhibits Showing Receipts and Disbursements, and the Applications for the Relief, with the Awards and Refusals of the Executive Relief Committee*. (Charleston, S.C.; Lucas, Richardson & Co., 1887), p. 4.

The damage caused by the Sea Islands hurricane to South Carolina's already poor economy was immense. The extreme winds and flooding did immeasurable damage to property, homes, businesses, crops and natural resources. Through many of the contemporary writings, the total assessed value for property damage is generally estimated at approximately ten million dollars. Ten million dollars in 1893 would be equal to approximately one hundred and ninety million dollars in 1998 terms.[93] In fact the traditional figures almost certainly understate the actual losses. Based upon the collected information, books, magazines, manuscript and especially newspapers, it seems more likely that the total economic impact of the Sea Islands Hurricane was over twenty million dollars in 1893 terms, or about four hundred million in 1998 dollars. The reasons are as follows: First, there seems to never have been an actual accounting, and when one adds up the

---

[93] To find the modern day equivalent two conversion formulas were used: Professor Robert Sahr's "CJR Dollar Conversion Calculator." *The Columbia Journalism Review.* Available from the Internet at: http://www.cjr.org/resourses/inflater.asp (April 1999), and S. Morgan Friedman's "Inflation Calculator." Based upon *Historical Statistics of the United States* (USGPO, 1975) and *Statistical Abstracts of the United States* (USGPO, 1976 – 1998). Available from the Internet at: http://www.westegg.com/inflation/ (April 1999). The "CJR dollar Conversion Calculator" computed ten million dollars in 1893 to be two hundred million dollars in 1998 dollars. The "Inflation Calculator" computed ten million dollars in 1893 as being slightly over one hundred and seventy-seven million dollars in 1998 dollars. Therefor, an average of the two is approximately one hundred and ninety million dollars.

daily and weekly figures given in newspapers accounts, the amount

is over ten million dollars. Secondly, it seems that shipping was

never taken into consideration; the ship the *John Kennedy* was a

total loss at three hundred thousand dollars alone.[94] Thirdly, the

loss of labor is another factor. Over two thousand dead is a large

loss in workers, farmers and field hands. Lastly, the loss to the

phosphate industry was massive and permanent.

The phosphate industry in South Carolina played a key role

in the State's economy. "During the entire mining era, 1868 –

1914, a total of 12,826,712 tons were mined... [and the number of

employees] must have been around 2,500 to 3,000 at its peak."[95]

The industry exported phosphate out of state while having very little

competition. The industry was monitored by the South Carolina

Phosphate Commission, whose agents would collect a "royalty" for

every ton mined and sold. Before the Sea Islands hurricane, the

phosphate industry "...paid in royalties nearly $600 per day into

---

[94] *The News and Courier,* 3rd September 1893, p. 1.

[95] Whitney, Richard A., *The History of Phosphate Mining in Beaufort County, 1870 – 1914.*
(Beaufort, S.C.; The Beaufort Historical Society, 1989), p. 18.

[South Carolina's] treasury, and expended thousands of dollars weekly in payment of labor..."[96]

Phosphate Towers and Processing Plant, Charleston, South Carolina[97]

With the exception of farming, the mining of phosphate was the largest industry in the State and the most important form of external revenue for its treasury. However, the industry was crippled in 1892 when phosphate deposits were discovered in Florida and South Carolina began to lose its outside markets to the competition. The deathblow came from the 1893 hurricane. "The

[96] Barton Clara, *The Red Cross, In Peace and War*, p. 210.

[97] Prints and Photographs Division, Library of Congress.

great hurricane of 1893 which swept over the Sea Islands destroyed many of the phosphate factories, barges, and equipment and in a few years the phosphate industry came to an end."[98] With the crippling of the phosphate industry and its near end along the coast, the industry and its supporters asked that the royalty to be reduced from one dollar per ton to fifty cents per ton. The royalty was reduced after the industry received a great deal of public support.[99] However, the industry was never able to recover completely. In *The History of Phosphate Mining in Beaufort County*, Richard Whitney sums up the demise of the industry as being caused by three events. The first was the recent discovery of phosphate deposits in Tennessee and especially in Florida. The second was the election of Governor Ben Tillman, who had been blamed for raising the royalty before the hurricane, and for mishandling the Phosphate Commission and the general economy of the State. Finally, on the 27th of August 1893, "...the terrible hurricane and tidal wave hit the area and constituted the crippling blow from which it never recovered.[100]

[98] McTeer, J.E., *Beaufort, Now and Then*. (Beaufort, S.C.; Beaufort Book Co., Inc., 1971), p. 86.

[99] The State, 3rd, 5th & 8th September 1893 and 21st October 1893.

[100] Whitney, Richard A., *The History of Phosphate Mining in Beaufort County, 1870 – 1914,* p. 19.

CONCLUSION:

"The Great Sea Islands Hurricane and Tidal Wave," as it was called, was a severe hurricane that produced such an extreme storm surge, so quickly and so extreme, it was erroneously described as a tidal wave, a phenomenon that typically occurs in the Pacific Ocean due to seismic activity. The "tidal wave" was truly a storm surge caused by the weather conditions of a hurricane and driven by winds over one hundred and twenty miles per hour. What made this event so catastrophic was that it hit during one of the highest tides for the Carolina coast since records have been kept. Therefore, a ten or fifteen foot storm surge on top of a ten foot tide created a wall of water well over twenty feet high. As in most hurricanes, it was the storm surge that caused the most fatalities and destruction.

With a twenty foot rise in sea level being driven onto the tiny Sea Islands by wind speeds over one hundred miles per hour, the water quickly covered the ground. Most of the islands were completely submerged and the residents were forced into the trees. The isolation of these individuals was shown by the simple fact that it took days before officials and the public even realized the seriousness of the disaster. When the real damage was understood, there seemed to be no one to offer meaningful help.

Luckily, Clara Barton and the American Red Cross offered their help albeit with limited funds (thirty thousand dollars). They set up by the 1st of October and continued to provide aid to the hurricane and flood victims until the end of June 1894. Despite criticism, limited resources, extreme conditions and problems caused by racial tensions during an age of lynching and racial brutality, the American Red Cross never let anyone die of hunger, thirst, exposure or disease.

All total the Hurricane killed at least two thousand people, and left thirty thousand homeless, their livelihoods destroyed and in severe need. The economic cost was approximately twenty million dollars, a devastating loss for South Carolina in 1893. The Great Sea Islands Hurricane and Tidal Wave, when loss of life and the numbers of victims are taken into account, is arguably the most disastrous hurricane ever to hit South Carolina and the eastern

Atlantic seaboard. Yet despite the magnitude of the disaster Congress did nothing, even though they had provided relief for other disasters. It is very obvious that both the Panic of 1893 and the race of the majority of the hurricane victims affected the situation.

Finally, South Carolina's most notorious Governor Ben "Pitchfork" Tillman was in office and became a center of controversy himself. Clara Barton and her biographers accused Tillman of asking for help from the Red Cross, and then later using the situation for political gains. Tillman, at least by 1894, was an easy target, already being demonized by the press, attacked for his racist and populist leanings. However, if one looks at the source materials in seems clear that Tillman was not to blame for the lack of relief and support from State and Federal resources. Perhaps (and despite his reputation as a "Jim Crow" Governor) he may have actually cared for the welfare of the black Sea Islanders.

Beyond the politics and charity of the day, the great question is if the Great Sea Islands Hurricane was the most destructive natural disaster and hurricane to ever hit South Carolina, then why are there so few accounts in any history books? One possible explanation was examined in an editorial titled, *The Public Interest in Disasters* in *Harper's Weekly*, the 16th of September 1893. The editorial suggested that the reporting of disasters was about drama and what makes interesting news. *Harper's* compared two August 1893 events, the dramatic cold-storage fire of Chicago that killed a very small number of people and the great Cyclone of the South Carolina Sea Islands. "That fire was intensely dramatic." "But there was nothing especially dramatic about the drowning of hundreds of Negroes on those low-lying islands in that gale."[101]

---

[101] *Harper's Weekly*, "The Public Interest in disasters" (16th September 1893), Page 879

The following transcription was made from an interview with Dr. Walter Edgar, conducted on camera in the Southern Studies Library and Reading Room, at the University of South Carolina on the 4th of April 2001.

THE AUTHOR

In general how would you depict the political climate of South Carolina in 1893 and the politics of Ben Tillman?

DR. EDGAR

South Carolina in the 1890's was a very turbulent place in terms of politics. Pitch Fork Ben Tillman from Edgefield County had upset the old Hampton-Led establishment in 1890, had taken control, firm control of the state government, had been re-elected in 1892 as governor. One of his platform planks was tremendous negrophobia. He attacked African-Americans in every possible way he could, and one of the reasons was because of the contested 1890 election. His opponent had appealed to black voters and so with African- Americans still being allowed to vote, they were going to perhaps cast the difference, or you know, cast the deciding votes in a contest between two white men and Tillman was going to see

that that never happened again. And two years after this, of course,

with his 1895 constitution, he would basically write African-

American voters out of the political process in South Carolina until

the 1960's.

THE AUTHOR

Could you please describe the race relations in 1893, and
more particularly, the political and economic status of black farmers
along the South Carolina Sea Islands?

DR. EDGAR

In the 1890's particularly in Beaufort and along the Sea

Islands, African-Americans were a tremendous majority. They still

held political offices, even in fact, despite Tillman. They held

political offices until the early 1900's, local offices only, not in the

general assembly, but local office, mayor, various school boards

and that kind of thing. The politics, they had was what they called a

fusion ticket. They would eventually in the 1990's, divide white

Democrats and black Republicans, and that was a way where the

party of African- Americans were Republican and what few whites there were in Beaufort County were Democrats. And the people in

Beaufort County seemed to get along together fairly well. Again,

because of the overwhelming black majority. It was more than

eighty percent African-American, close to ninety percent African-

American in Beaufort County.

THE AUTHOR

After the 1893 hurricane struck the Sea Islands, the US

Congress and State of South Carolina provided very little help in

assisting the victims of the storm. Also, despite Governor Tillman

convincing Clara Barton and the Red Cross to come and provide

relief, the organization was chastised for giving handouts and

making the victims "to dependent upon aid". Can you explain why

there was such opposition in providing relief to the hurricane

victims?

DR. EDGAR

Well the 1893 hurricane is one of those events; we know a

fair amount about it. As with most of those affected, they were not

literate, so they didn't leave a written record of their experiences.

There is a strong oral tradition in the black community and the Sea

Islands. The great storm of 1893, at first, after it hit people didn't know how bad it really was. I mean, literally, thousands; they estimate maybe three thousand, maybe more drowning. Many of them poor black farmers along the Sea Islands. They had no connection with the mainland and just literally disappeared. Then when, everybody's home got leveled and barns were leveled, and the town of Beaufort was hit pretty hard, people understood the extent of the disaster. But we didn't have a FEMA back in 1890 and state government didn't believe in helping anybody... much. And you had the other part of the equation, and that was the fact that most of the victims were African-Americans.

Now part of the opposition to what Clara Barton and the Red Cross was doing, and Tillman went on record with this, was-it was like, the Freedman's Bureau, it was giving all these black people free food and they'll be coming together, they'll cause trouble. Never once thinking of treating then as human beings who were suffering from this terrible disaster. This hurricane, the 1911 hurricane, the earthquake on Charleston in 1886, all within about 25 years, were a series of terrible natural disasters.

THE AUTHOR

The Sea Islands hurricane of 1893 was arguably the worse natural disaster to affect South Carolina, not to mention the second deadliest hurricane in United States history. Why do you think so little has been documented about this storm?

DR. EDGAR

After the Galveston hurricane, course, it was the greatest hurricane to hit the United States in terms of death toll. As I said before, at least three thousand people lost their lives, maybe more, we'll never know. One of the reasons it has not been well documented, part of it has to do with the times. You did have a couple of local newspapers and that sort of thing, but many of the people affected by the storm were illiterate, they didn't leave a written account of the storm. I think, as I mentioned earlier, in the African-American community of the Sea Islands, there was a very strong remembrance, memory, an oral tradition if you will, of the great hurricane of 1893. But in terms of the rest of the state, because Beaufort was isolated, literally in those days, the storm made it even more so. I think between the isolation and who was affected, people haven't paid much attention to it.

Now it most accounts of 19th Century South Carolina, you will find a reference to the storm. You can certainly find references to other hurricanes in books and in books on hurricanes it's mentioned. I mean that the 1893 hurricane is always listed because of the size of the death toll. The property losses were not all that great, not anything in comparison with even contemporary dollars, as say Hugo was. But, the loss of human life was just incredible.

THE AUTHOR

In the 1890's, the two main industries in South Carolina were farming and phosphate mining. The hurricane of 1893 caused significant damage to the phosphate mines and plants and the industry came to a close by 1900. Could you explain what effects the storm had on the phosphate industry and how it contributed to its demise?

DR. EDGAR

The phosphate industry in South Carolina, phosphates of course being used to make fertilizers, was one of the bright spots economically in South Carolina after the Civil War. Yes, you were planting rice, and truck farming in this area of South Carolina, down around Beaufort and Port Royal. There was no industry other than the phosphates and in the 1890's, three things actually hit the phosphate industry. One was the hurricane of 1893, which really, damaged the mines and plants tremendously. The other was the fact that Ben Tillman put a much heavier extraction tax on the phosphates and made them look elsewhere. And, what they did, they went to Florida and found huge phosphate deposits they could mine more economically and by 1900, that combination of forces had driven the phosphate business out, it had moved mostly to Florida.

BIBLIOGRAPHY:

Works Cited:

1. Barton, Clara. *The Red Cross in Peace and War*. Washington, D.C.: American Historical Press, 1904.

2. Burn, Billie. *An Island Named Daufuskie.* Spartanburg, S.C.; The Reprint Company, 1991.

3. Charleston City Council. *The Earthquake, 1886; Exhibits Showing Receipts and Disbursements, and the Applications for the Relief, with the Awards and Refusals of the Executive Relief Committee.* Charleston, S.C.; Lucas, Richardson & Co., 1887.

4. Congressional Record: Containing The Proceedings and Debates of the fifty-third Congress, first Session. Also, Special Session of the Senate, Volume XXV Washington; Government Printing Office, 1893.

5. Culp, D.W., ed. Twentieth Century Negro Literature; Naperville, IL: J.L. Nichols & Co., 1902.

6. Dabbs, Edith M. *Sea Island Diary, A History of St. Helena Island.* Spartanburg, S.C.: The Reprint Company, 1983.

7. Dulles, Foster Rhea. *The American Red Cross, A History*. New York: Harper & Brothers Publishers, 1950.

8. Elkinton, Joseph S. *Selections from the diary and Correspondence of Joseph S. Elkinton, 1830 – 1905.* Philadelphia: Press of The Leeds & Biddle Co., 1913.

9. Friedman, S. Morgan. "Inflation Calculator." Based upon *Historical Statistics of the United States* (USGPO, 1975) and *Statistical Abstracts of the United States* (USGPO, 1976 – 1998). Available from the Internet at: http://www.westegg.com/inflation/ April 1999.

10. Fox, William Price. Lunatic Wind, Surviving the Storm of the Century. Chapel Hill, N.C.: Algonquin Books of Chapel Hill, 1992.

11. Hamilton, Elizabeth Verner. *Storm Center*. Charleston, South Carolina: Tradd Street Press, 1983.

12. *Harper's Weekly.* "The Public Interest in disasters" September 16, 1893.

13. *Harper's Weekly.* "The Recent Cyclone in the South" June 9, 1894.

14. Harris, Joel Chandler. "The Sea Island Hurricanes, The Devastation." *Scribner's Magazine,* February 1894.

15. Hurd, Charles, Illustrations by Gil Walker. *The Compact History of the American Red Cross.* New York: Hawthorn Books, Inc.

16. Mather, Mrs. R. C. *The Storm Swept Coast of South Carolina.* Woonsocket, R.I.: C. E. Cook, printer, 1894.

17. McTeer, J.E. *Beaufort, Now and Then.* Beaufort, S.C.; Beaufort Book Co., Inc., 1971.

18. Mulloy, Robert. *Charleston, A Gracious Heritage.* New York & London; D. Appleton-Century Company, Inc., [date unknown].

19. Myers, Vance A. *Storm Tide Frequencies on the South Carolina Coast*; NOAA Technical Report NWS-1. Office of Hydrology. Silver Spring, Maryland; National Oceanic and Atmospheric Administration, June 1975.

20. National Oceanic and Atmospheric Administration Home Page. *Hurricane and Tropical Storm Data 1600 – Present… Georgia and South Carolina Storms*. Available from http://wchs.csc.noaa.gov/hurrican.html; Internet, April 1999.

21. *News and Courier (The)*. Charleston, South Carolina. August 28 & 29, 1893, September 3, 6, 7 & 8, 1893, and June 1 & 23, 1894

22. *New York Times (The)*. New York, NY. August 29, 1893.

23. Pryor, Elizabeth Brown. *Clara Barton, Professional Angel*. Philadelphia: University of Pennsylvania Press, 1987.

24. Rappaport, Edward N. & Fernandez-Partagas, Jose. *The Deadliest Atlantic Tropical Cyclones, 1492 – Present*. (Washington, D.C.: NOAA Technical Memorandum, NWS NHC 47, January 1995).

25. Sahr, Robert. "CJR Dollar Conversion Calculator." *The Columbia Journalism Review*. Available from the Internet at: http://www.cjr.org/resourses/inflater.asp April 1999.

26. *State (The)*. Columbia, South Carolina. August 29, 31, 1893, September 1, 3, 5, 6, 8, 12, 16, 18, 19, 1893, October 21, 1893, June 2, 1894 and July 23, 1894.

27. Stovall, Pleasant A. "The Cyclone in the South." *Harper's Weekly* September 16, 1893.

28. Tillman, Benjamin R., Governor (1890-1894), *Executive Proclamations; 1890 – 1894*. Special Collections and Manuscripts, South Carolina Department of Archives and History, Columbia, S.C.; call number S526003.

29. Tillinghast, B. F. "The Present and the Future of the Carolina Sea Islanders." *Harper's Weekly* June 9, 1894.

30. *Times (The)*. London. August 31, 1893.

31. Vietor, Daniel. *Hurricane / Tropical Data, Atlantic Hurricane Tracking Data by Year, Tropical Cyclone Data for 1893*. West Lafayette IN: Dept of Earth & Atmospheric Sciences, Purdue University. Available from http://wxp.atms.purdue.edu/hur_atlantic/1893/; Internet, April 1999. See "Hurricane No. 6 – Storm Track, August 15 – September 2, 1893."

32. Wetterau, Bruce, ed. *The New York Public Library Book of Chronologies*. New York: Simon & Schuster, Inc., 1990.

33. Williams, Sophia Wells Royce. "Miss Clara Barton and the Red Cross, A Study of Relief Work and of Agencies to Meet the Suffering from War, Pestilence and Catastrophe." *The Review of Reviews,* March 1894.

34. Whitney, Richard A. *The History of Phosphate Mining in Beaufort County, 1870 – 1914*. Beaufort, S.C.; The Beaufort Historical Society, 1989.

Additional Works Consulted:

1. American National Red Cross. Southeastern Area. *Hurricane Gracie Strikes in South Carolina, September 29, 1959.* Washington, DC: American Red Cross, 1959.

2. Christensen, Frederik Holmes, 1877-1944 (Diary). Special Collections and Manuscripts, South Carolina Department of Archives and History, Columbia, S.C., Manuscripts P+D4.

3. Deas, Anne Simons. Anne Simmons Deas papers, 1893. Special Collections and Manuscripts, South Carolina Department of Archives and History, Columbia, S.C. Manuscripts P.

4. Grimball, John Berkley, 1800-1893. John Berkley Grimball Papers, 1801. Special Collections and Manuscripts, South Carolina Department of Archives and History, Columbia, S.C. Manuscripts Pob.

5. National Hurricane Center. "Hurricane Mitch: One of the Deadliest Storms." *USAToday* On-line. Available from http://usatoday.com/weather/hurricane/1998/wdeadliest.atml; Internet, April 1999.

6. *New York Times (The).* New York, NY. August 28 – October 1, 1893.

7. *News and Courier (The).* Charleston, South Carolina. August 28 – November 1893 and May- July, 1894.

8. Snowden, Yates. *History of South Carolina.* Volumes I, II, III, IV & V. Chicago: The Lewis Publishing Company, 1920.

9. *State (The).* Columbia, South Carolina. August 28 – November 1893 and May- July, 1894.

10. *Times (The),* London. August 29 – October 1, 1893.

11. Wallace, David Duncan. *The History of South Carolina.* Volumes I, II, III & IV. New York: The American Historical Society, 1934.

NOTES:

The author of this book wishes to thank the following people for their support and assistance in the research, fact checking, encouragement and support: Dr. Walter Edgar, Dr. Kendrick A. Clements, Dr. Ken Peters, Dr. Walter Hanclosky, the wonderful staff of the South Carolineana Library, Thomas Cooper Library, the unknown technical support person at the Library of Congress who helped me out, Colleen D. Metts, Robert and Sylvia Dolan, George and Sandra Metts, Clara Barton, and finally to the memory of my good friend and mentor Dr. Ronald Baughman.